© Really Useful Map Company (HK) Ltd.
Published by Robert Frederick Ltd.
4 North Parade Bath, England.
First Published: 2005

All images © istockphoto.com

MYTHS AND LEGENDS

GODS & GODDESSES

CONTENTS

GODS OF THE WORLD

Religion has always been an important part of man's life. From the beginning, man has tried to explain the mysterious and the unexplainable through gods and religion. Ancient people believed that all elements of nature were part of a supernatural being. They attributed every event to this being.

 ## MULTITUDE OF GODS

Most ancient cultures believed in a pantheon of gods and goddesses. The ancient people believed that each god was given a particular responsibility. There were specific gods who represented specific aspects of daily life, including rain, harvest, the Sun, the Moon, wind and other forces of nature. All ancient cultures believed in gods of death and the underworld (hell). They believed that bad things happened when the gods were not happy with them, and so it was important to please and honour them appropriately.

Cerberus, the three-headed dog who guarded the entrance to Hell, was much loved by Hades, the Greek god of the underworld

CREATORS OF THE UNIVERSE

The ancient people were in awe of all that happened around them. They tried to explain everything, including their existence, through religion. Every culture in the world has a myth to explain the creation of the world and mankind. Some ancient cultures believed that in the beginning there was nothing. A few others described the early Universe as a great body of water. In the beginning of creation, god made the sky and land. Soon other gods appeared and they created mankind as well as other animals and plants.

HUMAN GODS

The gods were not only believed to be powerful and all-knowing, they were also imbued with human emotions. Gods of the ancient people were capable of making mistakes, losing their temper, and playing practical jokes on each other. Like humans, they, too, fell in love as well as fought against each other. Ancient mythology is full of stories about how the gods lived and – sometimes – died!

GODDESSES

The ancient people also believed that their gods had female counterparts. Most goddesses were regarded as the wives of the gods, but that was not their only identity. All goddesses were attributed with their own powers and responsibilities. They, too, were worshipped and were equally respected. In fact, in some places like India and Japan, certain goddesses were considered to be more powerful and, therefore, given more importance.

Lord Krishna of Hindu mythology was believed to have 16,000 wives! Krishna, who was another form of Lord Vishnu, died after being shot in the foot by an arrow

The revered Hindu goddess of wealth and good fortune, Lakshmi

MYTH

A myth is a story about the beliefs and traditions of a particular culture. It contains religious and magical explanations for events of the past. Myths try to answer questions like how the Earth came into being, and the role of gods in creating the Universe. Legends are stories that talk about a historical event and they could be partially or even fully true. The adventures of Robin Hood and King Arthur are examples of legends.

THE GODS OF ANCIENT EGYPT

The ancient Egyptians were very religious and believed in many gods. They had about 2,000 gods and goddesses. Some were worshipped all over the country, while others were local gods. Egyptians also believed that nature represented their gods. The gods themselves were often shown as humans with the heads of animals.

Atum, the creator god, also represented the setting Sun, and in this form was associated with Ra, the Sun god

THE COMPLETE ONE

Egyptians believed that at first there was nothing but a dark, never-ending ocean called Nun (or Nu). Then one day a piece of land emerged out of Nun. This land was called Ben-Ben and on it stood the first god, Atum, who then spat out Shu, the god of air, and Tefnut, the goddess of rain. Atum, the creator god, was considered to have both male and female qualities. He could therefore give birth to other gods. Egyptians often referred to Atum as the 'Great He-She'. His name itself means 'the complete one'.

NUT AND GEB

Shu and Tefnut had two children, Geb, the god of Earth, and Nut, the goddess of sky. Nut was depicted as arched over the Earth, touching the ground with her hands and feet. Her hands and feet were the four pillars that supported the sky. She was held up by her father Shu, while her husband, Geb, remained on the ground reclining on his elbow with the knees raised up. Nut and Geb had four children – Osiris, Isis, Seth and Nephthys.

Shu holding up Nut, the sky. It was believed that the day Shu was removed from his position, chaos would return to the world

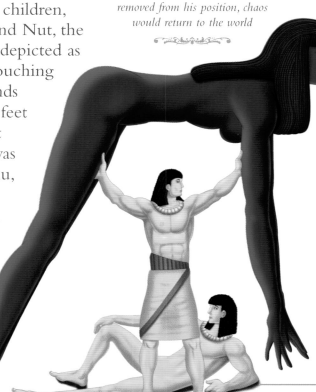

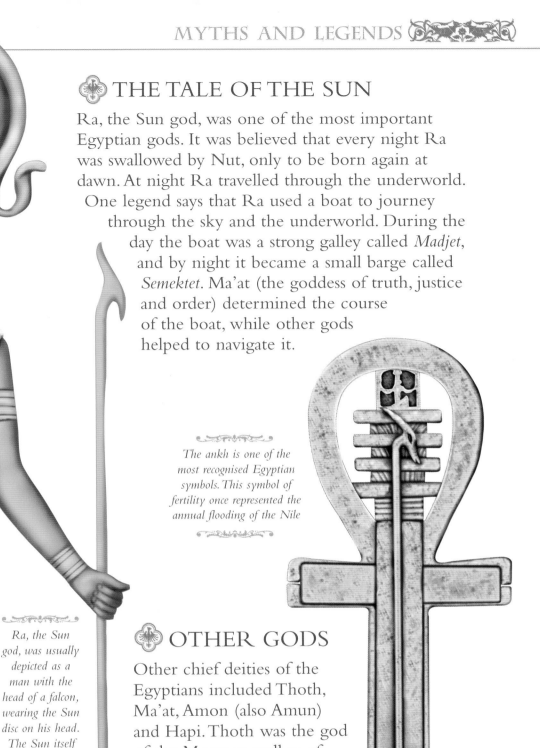

THE TALE OF THE SUN

Ra, the Sun god, was one of the most important Egyptian gods. It was believed that every night Ra was swallowed by Nut, only to be born again at dawn. At night Ra travelled through the underworld. One legend says that Ra used a boat to journey through the sky and the underworld. During the day the boat was a strong galley called *Madjet*, and by night it became a small barge called *Semektet*. Ma'at (the goddess of truth, justice and order) determined the course of the boat, while other gods helped to navigate it.

The ankh is one of the most recognised Egyptian symbols. This symbol of fertility once represented the annual flooding of the Nile

Ra, the Sun god, was usually depicted as a man with the head of a falcon, wearing the Sun disc on his head. The Sun itself was thought to be the eye of Ra

OTHER GODS

Other chief deities of the Egyptians included Thoth, Ma'at, Amon (also Amun) and Hapi. Thoth was the god of the Moon as well as of wisdom and learning. He and his wife Ma'at had eight children. Amon was the king of the gods and the most powerful too. Hapi was the god of the Nile. The annual flooding of the river, depositing rich soil on the banks, was considered to be the work of Hapi.

OSIRIS AND SETH

Osiris, the son of Nut and Geb, influenced the life and beliefs of ancient Egyptians more than any other god. He was the god of fertility, agriculture and rebirth, and the ruler of the underworld. He was also considered to be responsible for the start of the Egyptian civilisation. In contrast, his brother, Seth, was thought responsible for all confusion.

ISIS AND NEPHTHYS

Osiris had two sisters, Isis and Nephthys. Osiris was married to Isis, the goddess of magic. Isis was also the mother of Horus, the protector of the pharaoh. Nephthys, the goddess of the dead, was married to Seth. It is said that Nephthys was unhappy that her husband could not have children. She took the form of Isis and tricked Osiris into having a child with her. That child was Anubis, the god of embalming.

THE GOD-KING

As the eldest, Osiris inherited the throne of Egypt from his father. The new king soon realised that his people were nomadic and uncivilised. Osiris decided to change all that. He taught his people ways to grow crops, how to worship the gods, and rules for them to live by. Soon Osiris became loved by all.

Ancient Egyptians led a nomadic life until Osiris taught them how to farm. It is also thought that barley, their most important crop, was a gift from the god

THE JEALOUS BROTHER

Seth, who was jealous of his brother's glory, began to plot against Osiris. One day, he cunningly got Osiris to lie in a coffin and sealed him inside. The evil brother then threw the coffin into the Nile River. The coffin travelled several miles before it was washed ashore near the city of Byblos. A tree on the shore slowly grew leaves and branches around the coffin until it was completely hidden. The king of the land was impressed by the size and beauty of the tree, and had it cut to build a pillar for his palace, but no man knew what lay within.

Osiris climbing into the coffin as Seth stands nearby watching eagerly

A NEW LIFE

Isis had a revelation about the tree and travelled to Byblos. There she finally had the coffin taken out, and brought it back to Egypt. Seth feared that his treachery would be discovered, so he cut the body into 14 pieces and scattered it around Egypt. Isis found the pieces and put them back together. She then used magic to bring Osiris back to life for one more time, so she could have his child. Afterwards, Anubis and Isis embalmed the body of Osiris to make the first mummy.

THE JACKAL GOD

Initially, Anubis was the lord of the dead. It was believed that when Osiris died, Anubis gave up his position as the god of the dead out of respect for Osiris. Ever since, Anubis was known as the god of embalming. He also guided new souls to the Underworld, where he weighed their hearts against the feather of Ma'at. He took to Osiris the souls whose heart weighed less than the feather.

Osiris transformed into an akh (spirit) and became the ruler of the Underworld as also of the afterlife

PROTECTOR OF THE PHARAOH

Horus, the falcon-headed god of the sky, was a symbol of divine kingship. The ancient Egyptians believed that the pharaoh was the incarnation of Horus – and so referred to their ruler as the 'living Horus'. Horus was known as the protector of the pharaoh and the ruler of the living.

A DIFFICULT CHILDHOOD

Horus was born to Isis after the death of Osiris. Ever since his birth, Horus led a secretive life. Isis was afraid that his uncle Seth, who had killed his father, would kill Horus too. She raised Horus on a floating island so that Seth would never find him. Despite all her efforts, though, Seth found Horus. He disguised himself as a snake and bit the child. When Isis found the lifeless body of her son, she was distressed. She carried Horus to Thoth, who drove the poison out to save him.

In art, Horus was depicted in many forms. One of them was Harpokrates, or the 'infant Horus'. In this form, Horus was shown as an infant on the lap of his mother Isis

The Eye of Horus represents an ancient Egyptian symbol of power and protection

EYE OF HORUS

When Horus grew up, he had only one goal in mind – to avenge his father's death. Horus gathered an army and declared war on Seth. During the battle, Seth tore the left eye of Horus into pieces. Thoth collected the pieces and restored the eye using magic. The 'eye' of Horus became the symbol of health, prosperity and protection.

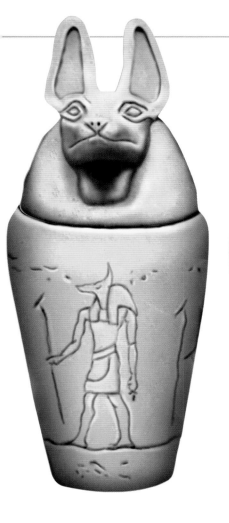

 RA'S JUDGEMENT

Once his eye was restored, Horus continued to fight. Both gods fought tirelessly for days, without either side winning. Finally, Thoth stopped the battle. He took both Horus and Seth to the council of the gods headed by Ra. All the gods, except Ra, agreed that Horus was the rightful heir to the throne of Egypt. Ra thought that Horus was too young and weak for such great responsibility.

Horus had four sons, Imset, Hapy, Duamutef and Kebechsenef, who represented the four directions. They also protected the canopic jars in which the organs of the dead were stored. Their heads were usually depicted on these jars

HORUS THE KING

Isis once again came to her son's rescue. She took the form of a young woman in tears and approached Seth. She told him that an evil man had killed her husband and was now trying to steal her family's fortunes. Seth became furious and declared that the evil man should be punished and the fortune given to her son. The moment he said this, Isis revealed her true self. Seth realised he had been tricked and was forced to give up the throne to Horus, since all the gods then decided in favour of Horus. Seth was banished from Egypt, while Horus became the king and united both Upper and Lower Egypt.

THE GODS OF ANCIENT GREECE

Like the Egyptians, the ancient Greeks also thought that their gods and goddesses controlled everything. Each god controlled one or more aspects of life and nature. The people made up stories about their gods to explain events that happened in their lives. These stories were in the form of poems and spread by word of mouth.

THE TITANS

The ancient Greeks believed that in the beginning the Universe did not exist. There was only darkness and void all around. They called it Chaos. From Chaos emerged Gaea, the Earth, and from her came Uranus, the Sky. Gaea and Uranus had several children, including the Cyclopes and the 12 Titans, or Elder Gods. Uranus was afraid that one of his children might destroy him and so held them prisoners inside the Earth. Angered by his actions, Gaea encouraged Cronus, the youngest Titan, to forcibly remove Uranus from the throne.

Atlas, who led the Titans against the Olympians, was condemned by Zeus to carry the world on his shoulders forever

A MOTHER'S SORROW

Cronus was a good king, but not a happy one. He was haunted by a prophecy, which said that Cronus too would be dethroned by one of his children. Cronus and his sister-queen, Rhea, bore the first of the gods and goddesses known as the Olympians. The Titan swallowed all his children as soon as they were born and kept them in his stomach. Soon, Rhea was about to have another child. This time she approached Gaea for help. Upon Gaea's advice, Rhea hid her son Zeus in a cave on Mount Dicte in Crete, and tricked Cronus into swallowing a stone instead.

HORN OF PLENTY

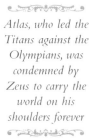

Zeus was said to have been fed on the milk of the giant goat Aega. The goat was very frightening to look at. Zeus, however, was not scared of the goat, whom he lovingly called Amalthea – after his favourite nymph. One day, Zeus broke one of her horns. Feeling sorry, Zeus blessed the horn with magical powers. It was then filled with whatever its possessor wished for, and was called the Horn of Plenty.

Rhea tricked Cronus into swallowing a stone by wrapping it in a blanket to look like baby Zeus

THE MISSION

When Zeus heard about his father's deeds, he decided to teach Cronus a lesson. First he poisoned Cronus, causing him to vomit up the children he had swallowed. Then Zeus and his siblings defeated the Titans and banished them to Tartarus, a cave in the underworld.

The nymphs took good care of baby Zeus. They even hung a golden cradle from a tree, so that the baby would remain suspended between the sky and land – and thus remain hidden from Cronus

A HIDDEN LIFE

Zeus was entrusted to the care of Adrasteia and Ide, daughters of King Melisseus of Crete, and of the goat-nymph Amalthaea. He was fed honey and goat's milk. Young warriors called Curetes clashed their spears and shields to drown the baby's cries, so that he would not attract the attention of Cronus. In this manner, Zeus was brought up in complete secrecy.

ZEUS – RULER OF THE OLYMPIANS

Zeus was the youngest child and so his older siblings were not ready to accept him as king. Zeus suggested drawing lots with his brothers Poseidon and Hades. Zeus won and became king of the Olympians. Poseidon became the lord of the sea, while Hades was made lord of the underworld. They were all called Olympians as they were said to have lived on Mount Olympus.

LORD OF ALL

Zeus was the god of sky. He was known to reward good actions, but was also often vengeful. This aspect is seen in the story of Prometheus, the Titan who fought on the side of the Olympians. Prometheus stole fire from the gods and gave it to man. This challenge to his absolute power made Zeus furious. He had Prometheus tied to the Caucasus Mountain, where an eagle tore at his flesh all day. At night, the flesh mended and the eagle started afresh the next day.

The Statue of Zeus at his temple in the ancient town of Olympia was one of the Seven Wonders of the World

MANY WIVES

Zeus was married to his sister Hera, but he had children with other women as well. He was the father of the younger Olympians and many Greek heroes, including Perseus and Heracles. Zeus often tricked women by changing his form. In one such instance, Zeus had an affair with Leda, wife of King Tyndareus of Sparta, in the form of a swan. After the union, Leda produced an egg, from which Helen of Troy was born.

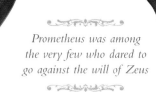

Prometheus was among the very few who dared to go against the will of Zeus

POSEIDON

Poseidon was believed to have had an unruly temper. When he was happy, the sea was calm; but when he was angry, Poseidon caused terrible storms and earthquakes. His temper is well depicted in Homer's epic poem, *Odyssey*. In the story, the Greek hero Odysseus blinded Poseidon's son, Polyphemus. An enraged Poseidon tried to punish Odysseus by bringing upon him fierce storms and terrible creatures, but Odysseus survived it all. Finally, Odysseus made peace with Poseidon by building a shrine to the god.

Poseidon was also the god of earthquakes and horses. He was often shown as an old man riding a fish

Hades carrying Persephone off to the underworld

HADES

Hades married Persephone, daughter of Zeus and Demeter, though she did not desire it. He had kidnapped her and tricked her into eating pomegranate seeds – after this, even Zeus could not free her. Meanwhile, Demeter's sorrow for her daughter caused a great famine on Earth. Hades agreed to allow Persephone to return to her mother if she would spend six months every year with him. Thus, summer and spring marked the time Persephone spent with Demeter, while her return to Hades caused autumn and winter.

THE YOUNGER OLYMPIANS

There were 12 Olympians in all. The elder ones were Zeus, Hera, Hestia, Poseidon and Hades – all children of Cronus and Rhea. The younger ones were Athena, Ares, Apollo, Aphrodite, Artemis, Hermes and Hephaestus.

THE WARRIORS

Ares, the god of war, was the son of Zeus and Hera. He was considered violent as well as cowardly, and therefore, not given much importance by the ancient Greeks. In contrast, Athena, the warrior goddess, was loved and respected. It is said that Athena sprang, full-grown and armoured, from the forehead of Zeus and did not have a mother.

A statue of Apollo, the god of youth, music and prophecy

THE TWINS

Apollo was the son of Zeus by the goddess Leto. Apollo had a twin sister, Artemis, the goddess of hunting. Hera, the wife of Zeus, was jealous of Leto. When Leto was about to give birth, Hera cursed her saying that she could not do so on land, in heaven, or on sea. Leto went around the world and eventually came upon the floating island of Delos. There she gave birth to Artemis, though Apollo caused her great pain. Hera had kidnapped Ilithyia, the goddess of childbirth, leaving it to Artemis to help her mother with Apollo's birth. Artemis was since revered as the goddess of childbirth.

One day a fight broke out between the goddesses Hera, Aphrodite and Athena over a golden apple. They approached Zeus, who in turn told Paris, a handsome young man, to judge the winner. All three goddesses tried to bribe Paris. Aphrodite, the goddess of love and beauty, offered him the love of the most beautiful woman on Earth, Helen. Paris promptly gave her the apple

GODDESS OF LOVE

The goddess Aphrodite was believed to have risen from sea foam. Another story says that she was born to Zeus and Goddess Dione. Aphrodite was so beautiful that Zeus was afraid she would cause the gods to fight. He had her married to Hephaestus, the god of fire, who was born lame. However, this did not prevent Aphrodite from having other lovers, including Ares.

MESSENGER GOD

Hermes was the son of Zeus by Maia, a nymph. He was the fastest among the gods and wore a winged cap and winged sandals. Hermes was also considered the messenger of gods. He was the god of boundaries and guided the dead to the underworld.

Hermes was believed to have invented foot-racing and boxing, and his statues were commonly seen in gymnasiums throughout ancient Greece

HEADY BIRTH

A popular legend said that Athena was the daughter of Zeus and Metis. Zeus had come to know that the child of Metis would be more powerful than him. He swallowed Metis, but it was too late. Inside his stomach, Metis began to make armour for her child. The hammering by Metis caused Zeus a lot of pain, and he had his head split open, allowing Athena to emerge.

THE GODS OF ANCIENT ROME

To begin with, the ancient Romans believed in gods without any human form. They were usually believed to be a part of objects or forces of nature, performing specialised tasks. Later, the Romans adopted many of the Greek gods, usually changing their names..

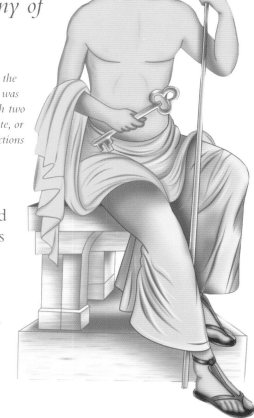

Janus was considered the guardian of gates. He was commonly depicted with two heads because every gate, or door, opens to two directions

OLD AND NEW GODS

Roman gods can be divided into two groups – the *di indigetes* and the *di novensides*. The *di indigetes* were the early Roman gods. They were minor gods who represented agriculture, fertility, home and grains. Of the *di indigetes*, only a few like Ops, Saturn, Janus and Quirinus were considered important. The *di novensides* were the foreigners. These gods were adopted much later, when the Romans came into contact with the Etruscans and the Greeks. Soon, the Roman gods were given human forms and stories were told about them. Some *di indigetes* like Saturn, Ops and Mars also began to be identified with Greek or Etruscan gods.

The temple of Saturn was one of the oldest holy places in Rome and was first dedicated in 498 BC

THE COUNCIL OF GODS

Like the Greeks, the Romans also had 12 main gods. They were called *dii consentes*. This council of gods consisted of six gods and six goddesses, led by Jupiter, or Jove, the Roman equivalent of Zeus. The others in the council included Juno (Hera), Neptune (Poseidon), Minerva (Athena), Apollo, Diana (Artemis), Mars (Ares), Venus (Aphrodite), Vulcan (Hephaestus), Mercury (Hermes), Vesta (Hestia) and Ceres (Demeter).

THE TRIAD

The Romans recognised three gods as the most powerful. These gods were Jupiter, Mars and Quirinus. Together they formed the triad. Jupiter, like Zeus, was the god of the sky and controlled the weather. Mars, the Roman god of war, was originally the god of agriculture. He protected the crops and animals from diseases. Unlike his Greek counterpart Ares, Mars was highly respected. Mars was also the father of Romulus, the founder of Rome, and his brother Remus. It was believed that Romulus later became immortal and lived as Quirinus, the third most important Roman god.

Romulus, the founder of Rome, and his twin Remus were the sons of Mars and his wife Rea Silvia. It was believed that Mars sent the she-wolf that nursed the twins

The sacred fire of Rome burned at the goddess Vesta's temple in Palatine Hill. On the first of March every year, the fire was put out and lit anew to mark the beginning of the Roman New Year

HOUSEHOLD GODS

Apart from the main gods, the ancient Romans believed in household gods called Lares and Penates. These gods were the escorts of Vesta, the goddess of the hearth. Penates were the gods of the storeroom. They protected the properties of the household. Lares were originally protectors of the fields. Later, they were given a place in the house. Every Roman family had one Lar, who usually was considered to be the spirit of a well-meaning ancestor. A small temple, called a *lararium*, was built in honour of the Lar. Some even thought Lares to be the children of Mercury, the messenger god, and a naiad (nymph) named Lara.

GODS OF THE CELTS

The Celts consisted of several clans, or tribes. Each clan had its own gods and goddesses. Some of them were common to all, but were known by different names. The Celts were highly religious people and took their gods and goddesses along wherever they went.

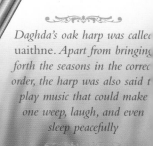

THE PRIMARY GODS

Most Celtic gods were considered to be the descendants of Danu, the mother goddess. Together they formed the tribe known as Tuatha Dé Danann. Daghda the Good was the chief of the tribe. He had a club that could kill nine men in one blow, a cauldron that never became empty, and a harp that called forth the seasons.

Daghda's oak harp was called uaithne. Apart from bringing forth the seasons in the correct order, the harp was also said to play music that could make one weep, laugh, and even sleep peacefully

THE MORRIGAN

Daghda had several lovers. Morrigan was one of them. She was depicted both as a single goddess and as a triad of war goddesses. The three goddesses who formed the Morrigan were Badb, Macha and Nemain. They often appeared for soldiers, washing blood stained clothes in the river, predicting which soldiers were going to die in battle.

AENGUS' DREAM

Once in a dream, Aengus saw a beautiful woman, Caer, and fell in love with her. Aengus decided to look for her. He heard that Caer took human form one year and turned into a swan in the next, and it was in the form of a swan that Aengus found her at the Loch Bel Dracon. Aengus also turned into a swan and together they circled the lake, singing a song. Aengus then took Caer back to his home.

THE SAINT AND THE LOVER

Among Daghda's children were Brighid, the saint, and Aengus Mac Og, the god of love. Brighid was the best known of all Celtic goddesses. She was so popular that the Catholic Church adopted her as the foster mother of Jesus Christ and made her a saint. Her brother Aengus was also a popular god.

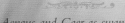

Aengus and Caer as swans. They sang a song so enchanting that all those who heard it fell asleep for three days and three nights

Lugh blinding Balor the giant with a stone

THE GOD OF LIGHT

Lugh, the god of light, was the son of Cian, of the Tuatha Dé Danann, and of Ethniu, the daughter of Balor, a Fomor giant. When Lugh grew up, he went to join the Tuatha Dé Danann. However, the gods decided to first put him to test. Lugh passed all of the tests and the gods finally accepted him. They also put him in charge of the battle preparations against the Fomor giants. During the battle, Nuada, the king of the gods, was killed by Lugh's grandfather, Balor. Furious, Lugh challenged Balor. The Fomor had a poisonous eye that usually stayed shut, but could kill anyone it looked upon. Thus, as Balor began to open this eye, Lugh quickly shot a stone into it, killing Balor and winning the war.

NORSE GODS AND GODDESSES

The Norse people lived in the region called Scandinavia, which includes present-day Sweden, Denmark, Iceland and Norway. In the 9th century, the Norse people known as the Vikings invaded and settled other places in Europe. Like all cultures across the world, the Vikings also had their own gods and goddesses.

THE WORLD TREE

In Norse belief there were nine worlds – Asgard, Alfheim, Vanaheim, Jotunheim, Nidavellir, Helheim, Niflheim, Muspelheim and Midgard. These were a part of a giant tree called Yggdrasil, or the World Tree. Ginnungagap, a vast emptiness, separated Niflheim, the land of ice, from Muspelheim, the land of fire. As the heat from Muspelheim began to melt the Niflheim ice, the drops of water that fell on Ginnungagap created Ymir, the first giant. With him also appeared Audumla, the divine cow.

THE BEGINNING

Audumla licked at the frost and salt around Ymir for food. Her constant licking caused Buri, the first man, to emerge. Meanwhile, a group of giants emerged out of Ymir's body. Buri had a son, Bor, who married Bestla, the daughter of one of the giants. Bor and Bestla had three children – Odin, Vili and Ve, the first gods. In the war with the giants, Odin and his brothers killed Ymir. From the giant's body, the brothers created the sky and Midgard, the land of humans. All the other giants, except Ymir's grandson and his wife, drowned in Ymir's blood, giving rise to rivers, lakes and seas.

Buri, the first man, is created as Audumla licks at the frost on Ymir, the giant

The Aesir burned Gullveig thrice, but each time she stepped out of the fire unhurt

 ## THE MAIN GODS

Odin, Vili and Ve formed the clan of Aesir, one of the main groups of Norse gods. The Aesir also included Odin's wife, Frigga, and his children, Thor and Baldr. Known as warrior gods, the Aesirs lived in Asgard. The Norse people also believed in another group of gods called Vanir. This group included the god of the sea, Njörd, and his children Freyr and Freyja, besides others. The Vanirs represented fertility and prosperity.

WAR OF THE GODS

The Vanir had among them a sorceress named Gullveig, who loved gold. On a visit to Asgard, Gullveig talked of nothing but gold. The Aesir tired of her talk and felt that such a greedy person should not live. So they threw her into the fire. To their surprise, Gullveig came out unhurt. The Vanir declared war on the Aesir. After fighting for years, the two groups decided to exchange hostages and end the war. Njörd, Freyr and Freyja joined the Aesir in place of Hoenir and Mimir, the wisest Aesir.

ODIN AND HIS SONS

Odin was the king of the Aesir gods. He was considered to be the god of war, death, wisdom, poetry, victory and hunting. He lived in a hall called Valhalla, or 'hall of the slain', at Asgard. From there he watched over the nine worlds.

ODIN THE OLD MAN

Odin was often depicted as an old man with a beard, wearing a wide-brimmed hat and carrying a staff. He had only one eye. He traded the other eye for a drink from the waters of wisdom in Mimir's well. Odin was usually accompanied by his wolves, Freki and Geri, to whom he gave all his food since he drank only wine. He also had two ravens, Hugin and Munin, who travelled around the Universe and gathered information for him. Odin also owned Sleipner, an eight-legged horse. Sleipner carried his master over the sea, through air, and to and from the land of the dead.

Odin with his wolves Freki and Geri, and his ravens Hugin and Munin

THE FINAL BATTLE

The end of the world would be marked by a final battle between the gods and the giants, called Ragnarök, or 'Doom of the Gods.' It would culminate in the death of Odin and his sons, and the end of the nine worlds. It was believed that Odin sent a group of maidens, Valkyries, to battlefields in search of warriors. The Valkyries brought back the bravest warriors killed in battles to Valhalla, where they trained for Ragnarök.

ODIN'S SONS

Odin was married to the sky goddess Frigga. They had three children, Baldr, Hod and Hermod. Baldr was the god of light and beauty. He once dreamt of his death. His mother became worried and made every creature and object promise that they would not hurt him. Loki, the trickster god, was jealous of Baldr. He tricked Frigga into revealing that only mistletoe could harm Baldr. Loki made a spear out of mistletoe and gave it to Baldr's brother Hod, who was blind. Hod threw the mistletoe at Baldr, who was killed immediately.

THE GOD OF THUNDER

Thor, the god of thunder, was the son of Odin and Jord, goddess of the Earth. Thor was often depicted as a strong man with a red beard and eyes of lightning. He protected both the gods and humans from the giants. It was said that thunderstorms were caused when Thor rode through the heavens on his chariot. He also caused lightning by throwing his hammer. It was believed that during Ragnarök, Thor would kill his biggest enemy, Jörmungand, the Midgard Serpent, but in turn would himself be killed by its poison.

Loki, the trickster god, guides Hod as he takes aim at his brother Baldr. Hod unknowingly killed Baldr with a mistletoe, and was in turn killed by Vali, Odin's youngest son, who was born specifically so he could slay Hod

THE GODS OF ANCIENT MESOPOTAMIA

Mesopotamia included the kingdoms of Sumer, Assyria, Akkad and Babylonia. Religion was important to the ancient Mesopotamians. Each town looked to its own patron god or goddess for protection. The people built pyramid-shaped temple towers, ziggurats, to honour their divinities.

SUMERIAN DEITIES

The gods and goddesses of Mesopotamia were Sumerian in origin. Later on, the Babylonians added new gods and changed some of the stories. According to the Sumerians, Nammu, goddess of the sea, gave birth to An, god of heaven, and Ki, goddess of the Earth. An and Ki had a son, Enlil, who became ruler of the gods. Enlil, called Ellil in Babylonia, was married to Ninlil, goddess of grain. Their children included Nanna, the Moon god, and Ninurta, god of rain and fertility. Nanna had three children: Inanna, goddess of love and war; Utu, the Sun god; and Ishkur, god of storms and rain.

Many archaeologists believe that Etemenanki, the massive ziggurat built in honour of the Babylonian god Marduk, was in fact the famed Tower of Babel mentioned in the Holy Bible

THE KIND GOD

Nammu had another son, Enki, the god of water, wisdom and medicine. The Babylonians called him Ea. Enki created humans and taught them arts and crafts. When Enlil and the other gods decided to punish mankind for their sins by sending a Great Flood, Enki warned the wise king Ziusudra (Utnapishtim in Babylonian). Enki asked Ziusudra to build a boat that would protect him, his wife, and a male and a female each of all animal species. Ziusudra followed Enki's instructions and survived the Flood.

A crown with horns was worn by Enlil and it symbolised his supreme power

ENUMA ELISH

In the 18th century BC, Babylon became the capital of Mesopotamia. Since the patron god of the city was Marduk, the Babylonians made him the chief god and also made several changes to Sumerian mythology. The creation epic, *Enuma Elish*, was written in praise of Marduk. In the epic, Apsu, the god of freshwater, and Tiamat, the ocean, produced the first gods, Lachmu and Lachamu, who were the grandparents of Anu, or An, and Ea. Each god had more children and soon there were several gods in heaven.

Marduk fighting the terrible dragon Tiamat. Marduk cut her body in two and created the sky and the Earth from it. Tiamat's tears formed the rivers Tigris and Euphrates

MARDUK THE MIGHTY

Apsu and Tiamat were so disturbed by the noise of the younger gods that they decided to kill them. But Ea found out Apsu's plans in time. He killed Apsu while he was asleep. An angry Tiamat created an army of monsters led by Kingu, her second husband. The gods turned to Ea's son, Marduk, for help. Marduk killed both Tiamat and Kingu. From Tiamat's body he created the sky and the Earth, and from Kingu's blood, the first man.

The Indian Trinity

The ancient Indians followed a religion called Hinduism, which continues to be the main religion of modern India. The followers of this religion are called Hindus. It is true that Hinduism talks about several gods and goddesses, but they are all different forms of the Supreme God, who is nameless and has no form.

THE CREATOR

The Hindus believe in three main gods – Brahma, the creator; Vishnu, the preserver; and Shiva, the destroyer. Together they are known as the Trimurti, or Trinity. One legend says that Brahma was born from a celestial egg. After his birth, Brahma began to create the Universe. In the process, he also created a beautiful goddess named Shatarupa whom he fell in love with. The goddess tried to hide from his gaze by running in various directions. However, no matter which way she went, Brahma developed a head to keep an eye on her. He grew five heads in total! Eventually, Shiva controlled Brahma by cutting off the head on top.

Brahma, the creator god, is often depicted with four faces, symbolic of the four Vedas – the Hindu sacred scriptures

THE DEVAS

Apart from the Trinity, the Hindus also believe in thousands of minor demigods called *deva*s. They are similar to angels and are believed to carry out duties on behalf of the Supreme God. The *deva*s are responsible for natural elements. They are ruled by Indra, the god of weather and war. Other important *deva*s include Agni (fire), Varuna (sea), Vayu (wind) and Yama (death).

Through his incarnations, Vishnu fulfils his role as the preserver of the Universe and restorer of moral order

THE GOD OF TEN INCARNATIONS

Vishnu is usually depicted as resting upon ocean waves, on the coils of the divine serpent Sheshnag. Vishnu is best known for his *dasavatar*, or ten incarnations. He is said to take up the form of animals or human beings in order to save the Universe from destruction. The gods Rama, Krishna and Buddha are regarded as incarnations of Vishnu. The last avatar of Vishnu is Kalki, who is yet to appear. This incarnation is often depicted as a man on a white horse holding a sword of flame. It is said that Kalki will destroy all evil and restore the good.

THE DESTROYER

Shiva is usually shown wearing tiger skin, with a cobra around his neck and holding a trident. The River Ganges flows from his matted hair, which is decorated with a crescent. One of his most powerful features is the third eye on his forehead. One day, Shiva's wife, Parvati, playfully closed his eyes. Suddenly, the world was plunged into darkness. A huge flame burst from Shiva's forehead and his third eye opened to light up the world again. Shiva usually uses the third eye to destroy the Universe from time to time, thereby paving way for new creations.

Lord Shiva was also known as Nataraja, or the 'king of dancers'

THE DIVINE MOTHER

Hindus believe that the Supreme God has both male and female qualities. Thus, the Supreme God is also worshipped as the Divine Mother, or Devi. Like the Supreme God, Devi also has various forms.

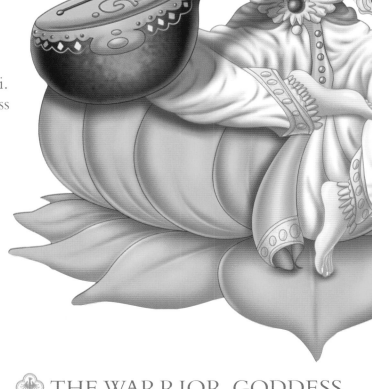

GODDESS OF WISDOM

The three main Hindu goddesses are Saraswati (or Sarasvati), Lakshmi and Parvati. Saraswati is Brahma's wife and is the goddess of learning and wisdom. She is pictured as wearing a white sari and playing a stringed instrument called a *veena*. Unlike her husband, Saraswati is widely worshipped in India even today.

Goddess Durga on her favoured mount, the tiger

THE WARRIOR GODDESS

Devi often assumes the form of an angry warrior goddess to protect the Universe. Durga is the most well-known of these forms. She was created to fight a deadly demon named Mahishasura, who could not be defeated by either god or man. Mahishasura had obtained a boon from Brahma that made him almost unbeatable. Soon he conquered the Earth, the heaven and the underworld. Realising that only a woman could defeat the demon, the gods created Durga. Armed with the most powerful weapon of each god, Durga killed Mahishasura in a battle that lasted ten days.

Goddess Sarasvati

🔱 GODDESS OF WEALTH

Lakshmi is the companion of Vishnu. She is the goddess of wealth, luck, beauty and fertility. She arose from the Milky Ocean, when the *deva*s and *asura*s (demons) churned it to obtain *amrita*, the divine nectar of youth and immortality. Lakshmi is also the mother of Kama, the god of love.

🔱 PARVATI AND GANESHA

Parvati is the wife of Shiva. Known to be a devoted wife and mother, her two children are Ganesha, the elephant god, and Karttikeya (also known as Skanda), the god of war. According to legend, Parvati created Ganesha using saffron paste. She then instructed him not to allow anyone inside while she bathed. Sometime later, Shiva came along. The boy refused to allow Shiva in and hit him with a staff. An angry Shiva sent his attendants to teach the boy a lesson. The small fight soon became a war between the gods and Parvati's son. During the battle Shiva beheaded him with his trident. Parvati unleashed an army of goddesses to destroy the gods, who suggested to Shiva that he replace the severed head with that of the first creature he came across. That creature was an elephant. Thus it was that Ganesha, the remover of all obstacles, got his elephant head.

Goddess Parvati creates Ganesha

MANDATE OF HEAVEN

China is a very large country. Each Chinese village and town had its own myths and legends, which were not recorded until the third century AD. The Chinese mythology we know today is a mixture of history and ancient folklore. It is also heavily influenced by the three main philosophical and religious systems of Taoism, Confucianism and Buddhism.

The yin is considered to be feminine and dark, and it represents night. The light and masculine yang represents day. The symbol shown here, called Taijitu, is widely used to depict the yin and the yang. Both yin and yang contain a little bit of the other. This is represented by the dots

A COSMIC BIRTH

The ancient Chinese believed that the Universe was created from a celestial egg. When the egg hatched, a Chinese giant called Pan-gu emerged from it. The upper part of the egg, called *yang*, rose to form the sky, while the lower part, *yin*, formed the Earth. With each passing day, Pan-gu grew taller and pushed the two parts further apart. About 18,000 years later, Pan-gu died. His eyes became the Sun and the Moon; his breath, the wind; his blood turned to rivers and seas; and his head became the mountains.

THE THREE NOBLE ONES

The three noble ones, or San Huang, were the god-kings who were believed to rule the Earth between the 26th century BC and 25th century BC. They were Fu Xi, Shen-nung and Yen-ti. Fu Xi is depicted as a human with a snake's body. His wife, Nüwa, created the first humans from clay. At first she painstakingly sculpted the figures. Soon she became tired, and dipped a rope in the mud and swung it around so that lumps of mud dropped to the ground. The crafted figures were the rich, while the lumps became the poor.

Fu Xi, one of the three San Huang

THE JADE EMPEROR

The Jade Emperor, Yu-huang, was the Supreme God who ruled over Heaven and Earth with the help of ministers. The emperor's court worked in the same manner as the Chinese emperor's. Each minister was given a particular task. Upon doing his work properly, the Jade Emperor would promote the minister. The ministers included the city gods, called Cheng-huang, and their assistants, Tu-di. It was their responsibility to protect humans against natural disasters. Zao Jun, the lord of the hearth, made reports about individual families, which he presented to the Jade Emperor on New Year's Day.

The Jade Emperor

The jade pi-disc represented heaven. The disc was placed on the chest of the dead before being buried. It was thought that the disc guided the souls of the dead in heaven

HEAVENLY RULE

The ancient Chinese worshipped their ancestors, who they believed mediated between human beings and gods. After death these ancestors were thought to serve in heaven's court. The Chinese also regarded their kings as representatives of the Jade Emperor. The kings were given the 'Mandate of Heaven' to rule. This was taken away if they became corrupt, and the mandate was then passed on to another person.

THE SUPREME GODS OF JAPAN

Most Japanese myths are based on ancient books like Nihonshoki *and* Kojiki, *which relate the origin of mankind and the history of Japan. Japanese mythology also relies heavily on folklores and the ancient Shinto religion. The word Shinto means 'the way of the gods'. Shinto gods were known as* kami.

THE BEGINNING

The Japanese believed that the world was created by Izanagi, the sky, and Izanami, the Earth. They stood on Amano-ukihashi, the bridge between heaven and Earth, and threw a spear into the ocean. When they pulled it out, the water drops that dripped from it formed into the first Japanese island, Onogoro. Izanagi and Izanami made this island their home and got married. They gave birth to many more gods and created the *ohoyashima*, or the 'eight great islands' of Japan. Their happiness was short-lived, though. Izanami died giving birth to Kagutsuchi, the fire god. When Izanagi heard the news, he killed his son in anger. He then went to Yomi, the underworld, in search of his beloved wife.

Izanagi and Izanami throwing the spear into the ocean to create the first Japanese island

IZANAGI'S FOLLY

When Izanagi found Izanami, he begged her to return with him. But Izanami had already eaten the food of the underworld and could not go back. Grief-stricken, Izanagi lit a fire to look at his beautiful wife once more. What he saw shocked Izanagi. Izanami's body was covered with maggots and worms. Terrified, Izanagi ran away from her. Izanami and the creatures of Yomi chased him, but Izanagi managed to escape. He closed the entrance to Yomi with a huge rock. Enraged and bitter, Izanami swore to kill a thousand people every day. Izanagi responded by promising to create 1,500 lives to replace the dead.

BIRTH OF THE SUN

After returning from Yomi, Izanagi began to purify himself. As he washed his eyes, Amaterasu, the Sun goddess, and Tsukiyomi, the Moon goddess, were born. Susanowo, the god of storms, was created from his nose. Izanagi then divided the Universe among them. Amaterasu received the heaven; Tsukiyomi inherited the night; and Susanowo got the seas. The Japanese believed that their rulers were descendants of Amaterasu.

THE HIDDEN SUN

Susanowo was always troubling his sister Amaterasu. Once, he scared her so much that Amaterasu hid in a cave – plunging the world into darkness. The other gods pleaded with her to come out, but Amaterasu refused. Eventually, Uzume, the goddess of joy, made the gods laugh so hard with her comical dance that Amaterasu peeked out of the cave. The gods immediately pulled her out and light was restored to the world. Susanowo was banished from heaven for his prank.

Amaterasu peeping out from the cave, where she hid to escape her brother's pranks

THE GODS OF LUCK

On the Japanese New Year, Sanganichi, people cleaned their houses and prayed to a group of seven gods called Shichi Fujukin, or the 'seven happiness beings'. These were the Japanese gods of luck.

 ## GODDESS OF GOOD FORTUNE

Benten, or Benzaiten, was the goddess of water, love, wisdom, music and good fortune. She was especially worshipped by geishas, dancers and musicians. She was originally a sea-goddess and only later became one of the Shichi Fujukin. Benten is depicted with eight arms, playing a musical instrument and riding a dragon. Two of her hands are folded in prayer, while in the others she carried a sword, a jewel, a bow, an arrow, a wheel and a key.

THE OTHER SHICHI FUJUKIN

Bishamon was primarily a god of war. As a Shichi Fujukin, he was also known to distribute wealth. He was shown wearing armour, with a spear in his hand, and standing on demons. Fukurokuju was the god of luck and long life. He is accompanied by a turtle and a crow. Hotei, a fat god with a big belly, was responsible for happiness and laughter. He was especially attached to children. Jurojin rode a white stag and was sometimes accompanied by a crane and a tortoise. He was the god of happiness during old age.

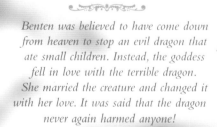

Benten was believed to have come down from heaven to stop an evil dragon that ate small children. Instead, the goddess fell in love with the terrible dragon. She married the creature and changed it with her love. It was said that the dragon never again harmed anyone!

*Daikoku and
Ebisu*

✦ DAIKOKU AND EBISU

Daikoku was the god of wealth and protector of farmers. He is
called the Great Black One and is usually pictured as a fat man
standing or seated on two bags of rice, with a bag of jewels on his
shoulder. He holds the magic wealth mallet in his hand. Ebisu, the
protector of fishermen, is regarded as Daikoku's son. Ebisu is shown
holding a fishing rod. A temple in Osaka was dedicated to him.

THE TREASURE SHIP

The gods of luck are Benten, Bishamon, Daikoku, Ebisu,
Fukurokuju, Hotei and Jurojin. They are depicted as sailing in
a treasure ship called *Takara-Bune*. This ship is said to come
to port only on New Year's Eve. The treasures include the
Purse with unlimited wealth, the Hat that makes its wearer invisible,
the Lucky Coat, and the Magic Key. The Japanese place pictures of the
Takara-Bune under the pillows of their children, so they have good dreams.

GODS OF THE ANCIENT AMERICAS

The continents of North America and South America are vast and rich in myths and legends. Religion and mythology were a way of life with the ancient Americans and helped them to explain many of the strange natural events that they could not understand. The mythology of the Aztecs, Incas and Mayans are particularly interesting.

The sculpture of a feathered snake from the temple of Quetzalcóatl in the Aztec city of Teotihuacán

THE GODS OF THE AZTECS

The main god of the Aztecs was Quetzalcóatl, who was depicted as a snake with feathers of a bird. The Aztecs believed that the world was created by the joined forces of Quetzalcóatl and his counterpart as well as rival, Tezcatlipoca. At the time, there was only the sea and a monster called Cipactli. Tezcatlipoca used his foot as a bait to capture Cipactli. The two gods managed to kill the monster, but not before it ate Tezcatlipoca's foot. The gods created land from Cipactli's body and filled it with human beings.

THE INCA GODS

The Incas believed that their first god Con Tiqui Viracocha emerged from a lake called Collasuyu. He also brought some humans with him. The god then created Inti, the Sun god, and the Moon and the stars. He carved more humans out of rocks and sent them to all corners of the world. But the people soon forgot about the god. Con became angry and punished them by spreading drought. The people had no food and suffered from heat. Inti's son Pachacamac felt sorry for the people. He forced Viracocha out and took over the Earth.

Yum Kaax was the Mayan god of corn. He was especially important to the Maya farmers, who considered the plant to be a gift of the gods

🜊 KINGDOM OF THE INCAS

Pachacamac had a brother named Manco Capac. The Incas believed that the god Inti sent Manco Capac and his siblings to Earth on a mission. They came out of a cave carrying a divine golden staff. Inti had told his children to build a temple to the Sun god at the spot where the staff sank. It is believed that the staff sank at the city of Cuzco. Manco Capac decided to build a temple at the site. He also established the kingdom of the Incas and made Cuzco his capital.

The famous Temple of the Sun, dedicated to Inti, the Inca sun god, is located at Machu Picchu, the 'lost city of the Incas', which was discovered in 1911

🜊 THE MAYAN GODS

In Mayan mythology, the world was created by Tepeu and Gucumatz, the chief god. One day, Tepeu and Gucumatz had a meeting with the other gods. They agreed that they needed to create a race of people who would worship the gods and keep their names alive. First they created the Earth with plants and animals. Man was finally made out of maize, after unsuccessful attempts with mud and then wood. Other main gods of the Mayan pantheon included Huracan, the god of storms; Ah Puch, the god of death; and Ixchel, the Earth and Moon goddess.

The temple of Kukulcan at the Mayan city of Chichen Itza. Quetzalcóatl, the feathered serpent god of the Aztecs, was known to the Mayans as Gucumatz, or Kukulcan

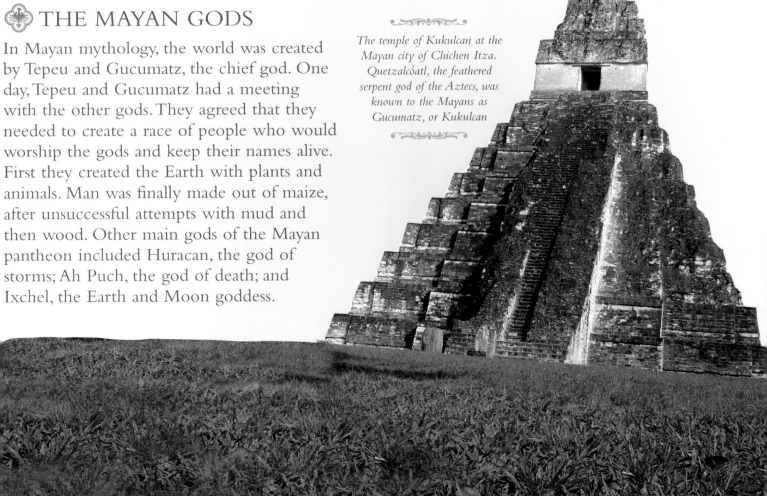

THE GODS OF THE ABORIGINES

The Aborigines were the original inhabitants of the continent of Australia. It is said that they arrived in Australia several thousand years ago by rafts and canoes. They spread across the continent and settled in small groups. Like most other cultures, the Aborigines did not have any written record of their myths and legends.

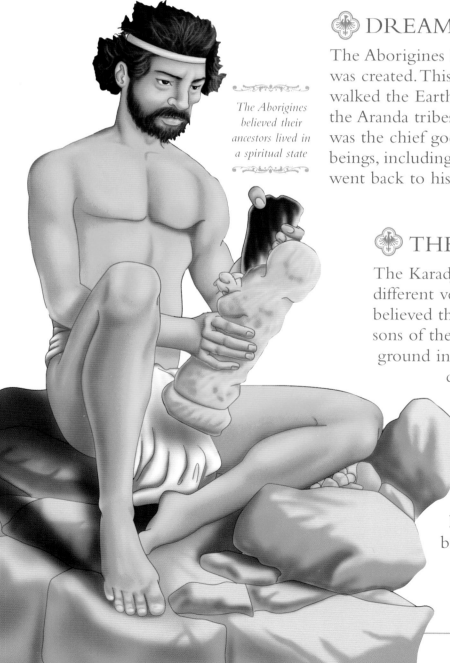

The Aborigines believed their ancestors lived in a spiritual state

DREAM-TIME

The Aborigines believed that nothing was real before Earth was created. This period, when the spirits of ancestors walked the Earth, was called the 'dream-time'. According to the Aranda tribes of central Australia, Altjira, the sky god, was the chief god then. He created the Earth and all living beings, including man. After his work was done, Altjira went back to his home and forgot all about his creations.

THE TWIN CREATORS

The Karadjeri tribe of northwestern Australia had a different version of the 'dream-time' story. They believed that two brothers called the Bagadjimbiri, sons of the Earth goddess Dilga, emerged from the ground in the form of dingoes. They set about creating the world. Afterwards they grew into giant men who touched the sky. One day the brothers quarrelled with Ngariman, the cat-man who lived in the sky. Ngariman was so angry that he had them killed. In revenge Dilga let her milk overflow, drowning the killers. At the same time, the Bagadjimbiri brothers were reborn. Later, the brothers decided to give up their lives. Their bodies turned into water snakes and their spirits became clouds.

Intricate Aboriginal art depicting religious motifs

THE ABORIGINAL SUN

Various aboriginal tribes had their own Sun goddess. Gnowee was one of the best known among the Sun goddesses. She is said to have lived at a time when people carried torches to light their way. One day, while Gnowee was picking yams, her young son wandered off. Gnowee began to search for him, but did not find him. However, Gnowee did not give up. She continued to carry a large torch and climb up the sky everyday in search of her son. Her torch was believed to be the Sun.

SOLAR DEITIES

Wuriupranili was a popular Sun goddess. Like Gnowee, she too carried a large torch believed to be the Sun. She walked across the sky from east to west with the torch. She dipped the torch in the ocean on the west, and used the dying embers to find her way back to the east again. The red-ochre paints that she dusted on her body created the colours of dawn and dusk. Other solar deities were Yhi and Walo.

The Sun goddess Gnowee's relentless search for her son with a torch is a popular Aborigine legend

GLOSSARY

Ancestor – A person from whom one has descended.

Aspect – A specific part or feature

Assume – Take on (the form of)

Attribute – To believe that a particular feature or thing is the result of some particular event or belongs to someone or something; a quality or characteristic of someone or something

Bait – food used as a trap for fish or animals, also something that is used to trap or tempt a person

Banished – Sent away from a place as punishment

Behead – Cut off someone's head

Boon – Blessing

Canoe – A narrow paddle boat that is pointed at both ends

Canopy – A roof-like covering over a particular area, throne or bed

Cauldron – A huge cooking pot made of metal

Celestial – Heavenly, belonging to the sky or heavens

Chaos - Confusion

Clan – Tribe, or a group of families

Corrupt – Accept money or reward to do something that is actually one's duty or against the law

Cosmic – Of or belonging to the universe

Cowardly – Having no courage or bravery

Deities – Gods or goddesses

Demigods – Lesser gods, or gods who are half-humans

Divine – Connected to god

Drought – A long time of no rain causing extreme heat and dryness

Embalm – To cover a dead body with special oil and herbs so that it would not decay

Embers – A piece of coal that is still burning a little, but without flame

Etruscan – A person from the ancient city of Etruria, which is now Lombardy in Italy

Fascinated – Find something or someone interesting

Fertility – State of being fertile, or able to produce babies or seeds

Folklore – Stories of a particular community, or place

Galley – A big, flat ship with one or more sails and up to three rows of oars. It was commonly used as a warship

Immortality – The state of being able to live forever and never die

Incarnation – A god in the form of a human; time passed in a particular bodily form

Inherit – To receive something (eg property, title or a even a quality or characteristic) from someone, often one's parents

Jade – A bluish-green precious stone

Lower Egypt – Ancient Egypt was divided into two parts – Lower Egypt and Upper Egypt. Lower Egypt lay in the north and was part of the Nile Delta where the river flows into the Mediterranean Sea

Mallet – A hammer with a big wooden head

Mandate – Permission to do something

Matted – Tangled

Navigate – To direct a ship or aircraft through a specific route; to follow a planned course

Nectar – Drink of the gods, or a sticky fluid produced by flowers

Nomadic – A life spent wandering without a permanent home

Obstacles – Troubles, or something that blocks the way

Painstakingly – With great effort, or carefully

Pantheon – A group of gods of a particular place or religion; a temple dedicated to all the gods, esp. the famous temple in Rome

Promote – To raise the rank or position of a person as a reward for his or her efforts and hard work

Recline – Lie back in a relaxed manner

Regret - To feel sorry for something one has done

Restore – To repair, or bring back to original state

Saffron – A yellowish-orange spice that is commonly used to add colour to food

Sibling – A brother, or a sister

Supernatural – That which cannot be explained, like ghosts

Triad – A group of three

Underworld – Hell

Unleash – Release

Upper Egypt – This part of Egypt lay south of the Libyan Desert and included the region up to Abu Simbel

Vengeful – A person who wants revenge

Void – Empty space

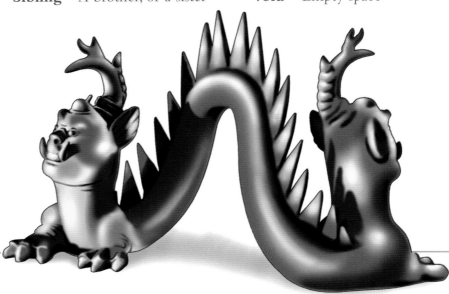